Cambridge **Discovery Education**™

▶ **INTERACTIVE READERS**

Series editor: Bob Hastings

# FAST

## THE NEED FOR SPEED

A1+

Genevieve Kocienda

# CAMBRIDGE
## UNIVERSITY PRESS

University Printing House, Cambridge CB2 8BS, United Kingdom

One Liberty Plaza, 20th Floor, New York, NY 10006, USA

477 Williamstown Road, Port Melbourne, VIC 3207, Australia

4843/24, 2nd Floor, Ansari Road, Daryaganj, Delhi – 110002, India

79 Anson Road, #06–04/06, Singapore 079906

Cambridge University Press is part of the University of Cambridge.

It furthers the University's mission by disseminating knowledge in the pursuit of
education, learning and research at the highest international levels of excellence.

www.cambridge.org
Information on this title: www.cambridge.org/9781107680685

© Cambridge University Press 2014

First published 2014
20  19  18  17  16  15  14  13  12  11  10  9  8  7  6  5

Printed in Dubai by Oriental Press

*A catalogue record for this publication is available from the British Library*

*Library of Congress Cataloguing in Publication data*
Kocienda, G.
 Fast : the need for speed : level A1+ / Genevieve Kocienda.
    pages cm. -- (Cambridge discovery interactive readers)
  ISBN 978-1-107-68068-5 (pbk. : alk. paper)
1. Speed--Juvenile literature. 2. Acceleration (Mechanics)--Juvenile literature.
3. English language--Textbooks for foreign speakers. 4. Readers (Elementary)  I. Title.

QC137.52.K64 2014
531'.112--dc23

                          2013018622

ISBN  978-1-107-680685

Additional resources for this publication at www.cambridge.org

Layout services, art direction, book design, and photo research: Q2ABillSMITH GROUP
Editorial services: Hyphen S.A.
Audio production: CityVox, New York
Video production: Q2ABillSMITH GROUP

# Contents

# Before You Read:
# Get Ready!

Why do things move fast? Sometimes, it's to catch food. Sometimes, it's to travel from one place to another. Sometimes, it's to race against other people. And sometimes, it's just for fun.

## Words to Know

**Complete the sentences with the correct words.**

speed

race

soar

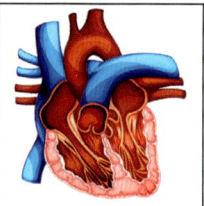
heart

**1** People, and most animals, have a _____.

**2** Cars _____ against each other to see who is the fastest.

**3** _____ is how fast something goes.

**4** When birds fly high in the sky, they _____.

**Read the sentences. Then complete the sentences with the correct highlighted words.**

This car can accelerate very fast. It goes from 0 to 100 kilometers an hour in three seconds! It has a lot of power. Very few cars can move so fast, but this car is not the same as other cars. It's special.

**1** When things go from slow to fast, they

_____ .

**2** When things _____ , they go from one place to another place.

**3** Something that is better than other things is

_____ .

**4** When something has _____ , it is strong and can move fast.

# CHAPTER 1

# What's Fast?

**THINK ABOUT THE WORD "FAST." WHAT DO YOU SEE? WHAT ARE THE FASTEST THINGS IN THE WORLD?**

Think about a group of horses running across green grass. Then think about a bird soaring through a blue sky. Now think about racecars speeding around a track.

What is the same about these things? It's **speed**. They all **move** very, very fast.

When you think about the horses, the bird, or the racecars, how do you feel?

Maybe you feel excited. Maybe you feel happy.

We love to watch things that move fast. We also love to run fast, drive fast, and swim fast. It is exciting and fun.

# What do you know about the fastest things in the world? Take the quiz!

**1** The fastest animal in the world is a fish. _____

   Ⓐ True

   Ⓑ False

**2** The fastest train in the world is in China. _____

   Ⓐ True

   Ⓑ False

**3** The fastest insect can fly at _____.

   Ⓐ 15 km/hour

   Ⓑ 35 km/hour

   Ⓒ 55 km/hour

**4** In the world's fastest car, you can drive at _____.

   Ⓐ 330 km/hour

   Ⓑ 430 km/hour

   Ⓒ 500 km/hour

**?** **PREDICT**

What other people, animals, or things do you think you are going to read about in this book?

Sail

fin

# CHAPTER 2

# Fast in the Water

**IT IS DIFFICULT TO RUN IN WATER. YOUR LEGS FEEL SLOW AND HEAVY. BUT SOME PEOPLE, FISH, AND THINGS CAN MOVE VERY QUICKLY IN THE WATER.**

The fastest animal in the water is the sailfish. It swims at 110 kilometers an hour. It is called a sailfish because it has a long fin along its back. This fin looks like a sail on a boat. But the sailfish doesn't use its "sail" to swim fast. When the sailfish wants to go fast, it puts its fin flat[1] on its back. Then it can move easily and quickly through the water.

The fastest sea mammal[2] is the orca, or killer whale. Orcas can swim at a speed of 48 kilometers an hour. Their speed helps them catch their food.

[1] **flat:** without high or low parts
[2] **mammal:** an animal that gives its babies milk from its body

Another fast animal in the water is not a fish – it's a person! In the 2004 Olympics in Athens, US swimmer Michael Phelps won six gold medals. In the 2008 Beijing Olympics, Phelps was the fastest man in the water. He won eight gold medals. And in the 2012 Olympics, Phelps won four more gold medals. He has more Olympic gold medals than anyone in the world – 18 in all!

Why is he so fast?

He has unusually long arms. From the fingertip on one hand to the fingertip on his other hand is 203 centimeters. This long wingspan helps him swim faster.

His feet are very big, and his legs are very long and strong. He can get more power with every kick than most swimmers.

Also, his heart is two times stronger than most other men's hearts.

Michael Phelps with one of his gold medals

Hydrofoiling

Ski

Most people can't swim like a sailfish, like a killer whale, or like Michael Phelps. But, we can all move very fast in or on the water. How?

We can move fast on the water by hydrofoiling. Hydrofoiling is a sport like water skiing. A person sits on a kind of ski behind a very fast boat. The person on the hydrofoil jumps and flips.[3]

F1 powerboats move very fast on the water, too. F1 powerboats are like Formula One cars. They go around a 350-meter course in the water. The powerboats speed around this course for about 45 minutes. They can go 240 kilometers an hour.

[3] **flip:** move your body so your feet are up and your head is down

Some people don't want to **race**. They just want to move fast on the water and have some fun. That's why many people enjoy riding on a jetski. They can speed across the water at about 100 kilometers an hour.

Other people want to move fast across the water, but they don't want to get wet.[4] For these people, there is the *Queen Mary 2*, the fastest cruise ship in the world. It moves at a speed of about 55 kilometers an hour. That's not as fast as a jetski, but it has restaurants, stores, and lots more!

[4]**wet:** when water gets on something or someone
[5]**snowshoe:** something big and wide put on a shoe to help people walk on the top of snow

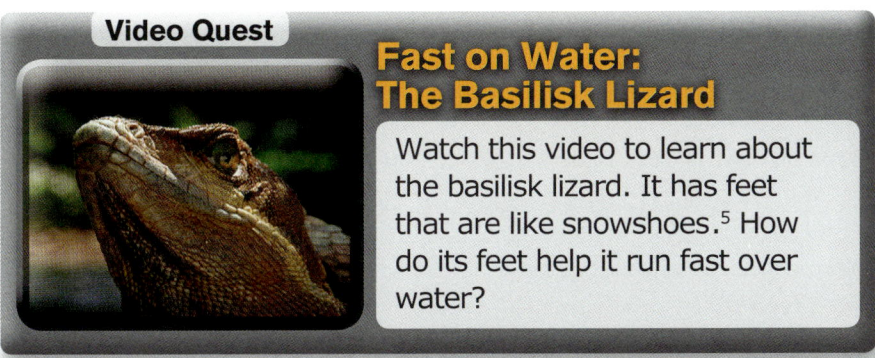

**Video Quest**

### Fast on Water: The Basilisk Lizard

Watch this video to learn about the basilisk lizard. It has feet that are like snowshoes.[5] How do its feet help it run fast over water?

# CHAPTER 3

# Fast on Land

**ARE YOU FAST ON YOUR FEET? OR DO YOU LIKE FAST CARS? LIKE MANY ANIMALS, PEOPLE CAN ALSO MOVE FAST ON LAND.**

One of the fastest runners in the world is Jamaica's Usain Bolt. When he was a young boy, he loved playing football. When he played, Usain's teachers saw that he was very fast. They wanted him to run in races. He came in second in his first school race in 2001, and in 2002 he became the world champion[6] in his age group.

In the 2008 Olympics in Beijing, Usain won gold medals in the 100-meter race, the 200-meter race, and the 4x100-meter race. And he set a world record[7] in all three races! Four years later, in the 2012 Olympics in London, he won all three races again. He is the first man in the world to win all three races in two Olympics.

[6]**champion:** the fastest person in a race
[7]**set a record:** If you set a world record in a race, you get the fastest time in the world.

How fast is Bolt? Very. He can run the 100 meters at a speed of 44.72 kilometers an hour. That's why he is called "**Lightning** Bolt"!

A lightning bolt

Usain Bolt is fast, but there are **land** animals that are much faster.

The cheetah is the fastest land animal. It can run 112 kilometers an hour. But that's not all. The cheetah can **accelerate** faster than any other animal. It can accelerate from 0 to about 100 kilometers an hour in only three seconds. That is faster than the fastest cars.

The cheetah is really fast, but only for very short **distances**. For long distances, the pronghorn antelope is the champion of the animal world. It can run at more than 86 kilometers an hour for short distances and at about half that speed for many miles. In a marathon, the pronghorn antelope will finish the 42 kilometers in less than an hour.

Cheetah

Pronghorn antelope

13

It doesn't take legs or feet to be fast. The death adder snake does not have legs or feet to run. It hides[8] and waits for its food. When a bird or other animal comes close, the snake moves its head really fast. The death adder can move its head and bite[9] an animal in less than 0.15 seconds. That's lightning fast. It's so fast that people can't see it bite! The death adder is one of the fastest, if not the fastest, snake in the world.

[8] **hide:** stay or wait in a place where no one can see you
[9] **bite:** cut into something with your teeth
[10] **get away from:** leave a place where you don't want to be

**Video Quest**

**Fast on Land: The Sand Fish**

Watch this video to learn about a special lizard. How does the sand fish get away from[10] the hot sun?

Do you need to go somewhere really fast? For $2,400,000, you can have the fastest car in the world. It's the Bugatti Veyron Super Sport, and its fastest speed is 430 kilometers an hour.

Or maybe you don't want to drive. There are many super fast trains in the world. The fastest one is in China. It takes only 3 hours and 58 minutes to travel between Shanghai and Beijing – a trip of 1,305 kilometers. The average[11] speed of this train is 329 kilometers an hour. If you take this train, don't bring a long book!

[11] **average:** not the fastest or the slowest; in the middle

A person speed flying wears skis and a parachute called a "wing."

# CHAPTER 4

# Fast in the Air

**PEOPLE TRY DIFFERENT WAYS TO SOAR LIKE BIRDS IN THE SKY.**

Many people fly in airplanes every day. What other ways do people fly? One way is called speed flying.

What is speed flying? It's a cool new sport that people around the world are doing. You need skis, a type of parachute called a "wing," and a snowy **mountain**. Speed fliers begin skiing down a mountain. When they are going fast enough, they can use the wing to fly over parts of the mountain. Speed flying is an exciting sport that lets you ski and fly. You can go fast on land and in the air!

Speed fliers fly very, very fast. A speed flyer can fly down a mountain at up to 145 kilometers an hour.

Speed fliers can go very fast, but they are much slower than the fastest bird in the world – the peregrine falcon.

The peregrine falcon lives in many places on Earth. It hunts[12] and eats other smaller birds. It can catch these birds at a speed of 322 kilometers an hour. That's three times faster than the cheetah!

How can they go so fast? They have very, very strong wings. They also have really strong hearts and lungs.[13]

[12]**hunt:** try to catch an animal
[13]**lung:** a part inside your body that takes air in and out

**?** **ANALYZE**
What is different about how people and animals fly fast?

# CHAPTER 5

# Sonic Boom

**SOMETIMES, MOVING VERY FAST MAKES A VERY LOUD NOISE. IT'S CALLED A SONIC BOOM.**

This pilot is breaking the sound barrier.

A sonic boom is a very loud noise that happens when something travels faster than the speed of sound.[14] Why does this happen?

Think about a boat moving on the water. There are small waves[15] in front of and behind the boat. But if the boat moves faster than the small waves, then the waves become one big wave.

The same thing happens with an airplane. An airplane has sound waves in front of it and around it. In the air, the speed of sound is about 1,225 kilometers an hour. When a plane travels faster than the speed of sound, the sound waves all come together and make one big sound. That's the sonic boom.

[14]**sound:** something you hear
[15] **wave:** some high water that you see on the sea, sometimes from boats

**Video Quest**

### Time Warp: Bullwhip

Watch this video about a sonic boom. What can make a sonic boom?

For a long time, people tried to fly faster than the speed of sound, but it was very **dangerous**. The planes did not have enough power and fell to Earth. Many men died.

Then in 1947, US pilot Charles "Chuck" Yeager flew a new kind of plane. He was the first man to fly faster than the speed of sound, the first man to break the sound barrier[16] and hear a sonic boom.

However, Yeager wasn't really the first animal to move faster than sound. Millions of years ago, dinosaurs made sonic booms. Some dinosaurs had very long, very strong tails.[17] They moved their tails very, very fast – faster than the speed of sound. Boom!

[16] **barrier:** something that stops a person or thing
[17] **tail:** the part of an animal's body at the end of the back

People bungee jump from something high using an elastic rope tied around their legs.

# CHAPTER 6

# What Do You Think?

**DO YOU WANT TO SOAR IN THE AIR LIKE A BIRD? OR DRIVE A CAR IN A RACE?**

Today cars, planes, and people are very fast. In 1897, a fast car traveled at only 45 kilometers an hour. Today the Bugatti Veyron Super Sport travels at 430 kilometers an hour. The Wright Brothers' plane traveled at only 48 kilometers an hour in 1903. In 1967 the X-15 set the speed record for the fastest plane with a pilot. It flew at 7,274 kilometers per hour. At the first Olympics in 1896, the winner of the 100-meter race finished in 12 seconds. Today runners like Usain Bolt can run 100 meters in under 9.6 seconds.

Do you like going fast? What's the fastest thing you ever did?

If you want to know what it's like to fly, you can try bungee jumping. First, you find a very high bridge. Then you tie an elastic rope to your legs. Then, you jump! The highest bungee jump in the world is from the Macau Tower in China. It is 233 meters high. Bungee jumpers travel at a speed of 200 kilometers an hour.

If bungee jumping isn't fast enough for you, maybe you'd like to drive a car at 300 kilometers an hour. In many places, you can go to special driving schools and learn to drive a racecar like your favorite driver.

Which of these two fast sports do you want to try?

**? ANALYZE**
What other things in the world are getting faster?

Wright Brothers' first Kitty Hawk plane, 1903

X-15 aircraft

U.S. AIR FORCE

NASA

# After You Read

Read the sentences and choose Ⓐ (True) or Ⓑ (False).

**1** The orca is faster than the sailfish.
- Ⓐ True
- Ⓑ False

**2** Michael Phelps won four gold medals in the 2012 Olympics.
- Ⓐ True
- Ⓑ False

**3** The *Queen Mary 2* travels at about 55 kilometers an hour.
- Ⓐ True
- Ⓑ False

**4** The cheetah is not fast for long distances.
- Ⓐ True
- Ⓑ False

**Video**
**5** The basilisk lizard can fly across the top of the water.
- Ⓐ True
- Ⓑ False

**6** The peregrine falcon can fly fast because of its strong legs and head.
- Ⓐ True
- Ⓑ False

**7** Chuck Yeager was the first man to break the sound barrier.
- Ⓐ True
- Ⓑ False

**8** A sonic boom is a very loud noise.
- Ⓐ True
- Ⓑ False

## Match

Match the vocabulary with the correct definitions.

| Words | Definitions |
|---|---|
| 1. soar _____ | a. fly high and fast in the sky |
| 2. speed _____ | b. try to be faster than another person |
| 3. move _____ | c. an important part of the inside of your body |
| 4. accelerate _____ | d. how fast or slow something goes |
| 5. heart _____ | e. better than other things |
| 6. power _____ | f. something that makes a person or animal strong and fast |
| 7. special _____ | g. go from one place to a different place |
| 8. race _____ | h. go from slow to fast |

## Answer the Questions

Read pages 9 and 12 again and answer the questions.

**1** How many Olympic gold medals did Michael Phelps win all together?

_____

**2** What is special about Michael Phelps' arms?

_____

**3** Which races did Usain Bolt win in the 2008 and 2012 Olympics?

_____

**4** Usain Bolt was the first man to do what?

_____

# Answer Key

**Words to Know, page 4**

**1** heart **2** race **3** Speed **4** soar

**Words to Know, page 5**

**1** accelerate **2** move **3** special **4** power

**Quiz, page 7**

**1** B **2** A **3** B **4** B

**Predict, page 7** *Answers will vary.*

**Video Quest, page 11**

Its feet are big and wide like snowshoes so it can stay on top of the water.

**Video Quest, page 14**

It digs under the sand.

**Analyze, page 17**

People use things like airplanes and wings to fly. Animals only need their bodies that are made to fly fast.

**Video Quest, page 19**

A bullwhip can make a sonic boom.

**Analyze, page 21** *Answers will vary.*

**True or False, page 22**

**1** B **2** A **3** A **4** A **5** B **6** B **7** A **8** A

**Match, page 23**

**1** a **2** d **3** g **4** h **5** c **6** f **7** e **8** b

**Answer the Questions, page 23**

**1** 18. **2** They are very long. **3** The 100-meter, 200-meter, and 4x100-meter races. **4** Bolt was the first man to win the 100-meter, 200-meter, and 4x100-meter races in two Olympics.